THE SECRET LIVES OF PLANTS!

BY JANET SLINGERLAND

ILLUSTRATED BY OKSANA KEMARSKAYA

Graphic Library is published by Capstone Press,
1710 Roe Crest Drive, North Mankato, Minnesota 56003.
www.capstonepub.com

Library of Congress Cataloging-in-Publication Data
Slingerland, Janet.
  The secret lives of plants! / by Janet Slingerland ; illustrated by Oksana Kemarskaya.
     p. cm.—(Graphic library. Adventures in science)
  Includes bibliographical references and index.
  Summary: "In graphic novel format, explores plant biology, including life cycle,
photosynthesis, transpiration, respiration, and reproduction"—Provided by publisher.
  ISBN 978-1-4296-7686-1 (library binding)
  ISBN 978-1-4296-7989-3 (paperback)
  1. Plants—Juvenile literature. 2. Plant life cycles—Juvenile literature. I. Kemarskaya,
Oksana, ill. II. Title. III. Series.
  QK49.S59 2012
  580—dc23   2011028744

Art Director
Nathan Gassman

Designer
Lori Bye

Editor
Christopher L. Harbo

Production Specialist
Laura Manthe

Consultant:
Kenneth M. Cameron, PhD
Director, Wisconsin State Herbarium
Professor, Department of Botany
University of Wisconsin, Madison

TABLE OF CONTENTS

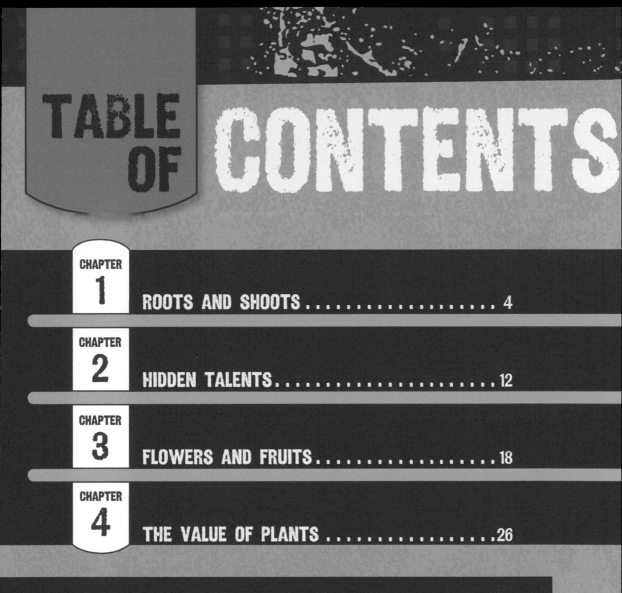

CHAPTER 1

ROOTS AND SHOOTS

A little acorn has found its way into a prime spot. Like all living things, this seed needs food, air, and water to grow. But our little friend also needs sunlight, time, and a whole lot of luck.

Uh-oh! A squirrel thinks the acorn would make a nice midwinter snack. Is this the end of our little friend?

The squirrel forgot where he buried his snack. This is a lucky turn of events for the acorn.

The acorn soaks up water and the warmth of the sun. It sprouts and grows.

FACT One mature oak tree can make more than 3,000 acorns in one year.

Whoa! Our little friend isn't little any more. Now a mighty oak tree, its roots spread out underground. Its shoots reach toward the sky.

SHOOTS

ROOTS

The tree spreads its roots for good reason. Roots anchor it in the soil. They keep the tree from falling over.

FACT
A plant's shoots include its stems, branches, leaves, flowers, fruit, and seeds.

Roots also absorb nutrients and water from the soil. They pass them along to the rest of the plant.

The tree's trunk is no slacker either. As the tree's main stem, the trunk supports other stems called branches. Branches hold buds, leaves, and younger stems.

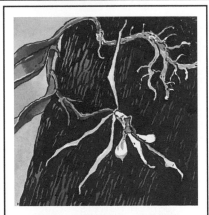

Stems hide the plant's plumbing system. Water and nutrients move around the plant through stems. Most plants keep their stems above ground. Some plants, such as potatoes, have underground stems.

WHO NEEDS SOIL?

Some plants don't bother to root themselves in the ground. Epiphytes such as orchids grip tree branches with their roots. They suck water out of humid air.

Plants keep secrets in their roots and shoots. Inside every plant, tiny cells are hard at work. Each cell is filled with organelles that keep the plant living and growing.

CHLOROPLASTS

A stiff cell wall protects and shapes each cell. Inside this wall, the cell membrane decides which molecules can pass through.

CELL WALL

CELL MEMBRANE

The hardest working organelles hide within the plant's leaf cells. Chloroplasts hold chlorophyll, a material that gives the plant its green color. Chloroplasts use the chlorophyll to turn the sun's energy into sugar during photosynthesis.

MITOCHONDRIA

VACUOLE

NUCLEUS

CYTOPLASM

When the cell needs to power up, mitochondria organelles get to work. They break down the sugar created in photosynthesis, turning it into energy the cell can use.

Each cell has to put its food, water, and waste somewhere. That's why it has a fluid-filled vacuole. This sack also helps the cell keep its shape. If the plant lacks fluid, the vacuole shrinks, and the plant wilts.

The nucleus controls what happens in the cell. The nucleus also holds the cell's DNA, the plant's genetic material. Outside the nucleus, a jellylike goo called cytoplasm fills the cell.

FACT
DNA stands for deoxyribonucleic acid. It holds the plant's genetic code. This code decides what features the plant will have. These features include plant size, flower shape, leaf shape, and color.

A plant's cells work hard doing different jobs. To make their jobs easier, similar plant cells join forces to form tissues.

DERMAL TISSUE

The easiest plant tissue to see is the skin it lives in. Dermal tissue is usually a single layer of cells. It covers a plant's leaves, stems, and roots.

Some tissues are construction zones. Within this bud, meristematic tissue makes the plant grow. As meristem cells divide and get bigger, the plant grows taller and stems get thicker.

MERISTEMATIC TISSUE

GROUND TISSUE

Ground tissue gives plants bulk. Different cells make up this plant-filling tissue. Ground tissue cells make and store food, hold water, and shape the plant.

Stems hide tubes made from vascular tissue. Water, sugar, and nutrients move through these vascular bundles.

Some plants scatter their vascular bundles throughout the stem. Others arrange their vascular bundles in rings.

VASCULAR BUNDLES

VASCULAR BUNDLES

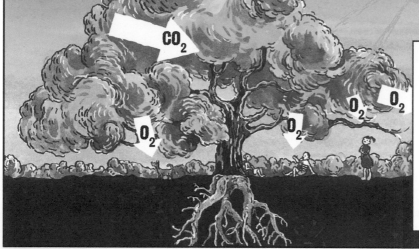

Once a plant has leaves, it can perform photosynthesis. This process turns sunlight and carbon dioxide (CO_2) into food and oxygen (O_2). Plants use the carbon dioxide people and animals breathe out. They make the oxygen people and animals breathe in.

To start photosynthesis, plants take in carbon dioxide through tiny holes in their leaves called stomata. Water and nutrients flow through veins from the stem to the leaf.

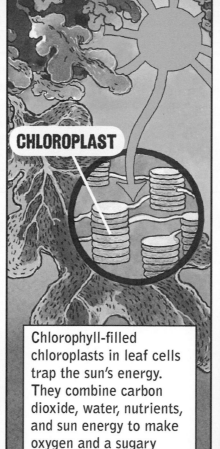

CHLOROPLAST

Chlorophyll-filled chloroplasts in leaf cells trap the sun's energy. They combine carbon dioxide, water, nutrients, and sun energy to make oxygen and a sugary plant food called glucose.

The stomata release the oxygen. The glucose moves through the leaf's veins to the stem.

GLUCOSE

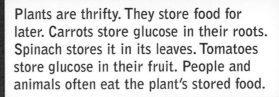

Plants are thrifty. They store food for later. Carrots store glucose in their roots. Spinach stores it in its leaves. Tomatoes store glucose in their fruit. People and animals often eat the plant's stored food.

Plants have another hidden talent. During transpiration, they take water into their roots. The water moves through stems and leaves. Then it is released into the air. Everyone knows plants need water to live. But 90 percent of the water they absorb goes back into the air.

WATER VAPOR

WATER

WATER

Of course, transpiration isn't just about moving water from the soil to the air. The water flowing through the plant carries nutrients and sugars around. The water pressure also helps keep the plant standing.

Transpiration makes plants "sweat." Water droplets exit through the stomata. The open stomata then absorb carbon dioxide for photosynthesis.

What happens when transpiration stops? The plant loses more water than it takes in. It closes its stomata to save water, so it can't perform photosynthesis. The plant dies if it goes without water for too long.

FACT Each day, a large tree can move up to 100 gallons (379 liters) of water from the ground to the air. That's enough for at least two baths.

For respiration to occur, the plant puts its roots and leaves to work taking in oxygen. The plant uses the oxygen to turn stored sugars into usable energy. The plant then releases water vapor through the stomata. It releases carbon dioxide through roots and leaves.

CARBON DIOXIDE

OXYGEN

WATER

CARBON DIOXIDE

OXYGEN

A plant's work is never done. Day and night, most of the cells in the plant perform respiration. The plant turns stored food into energy it can use to live, grow, and flower.

Respiration reverses some of the effects of photosynthesis. During photosynthesis, plants take in carbon dioxide and give off oxygen. During respiration, they take in oxygen and give off carbon dioxide. Each day, the amount of sunlight drives how much carbon dioxide and oxygen are absorbed and released. In the end, plants replace enough carbon dioxide with oxygen for people and animals to breathe the air.

PLANT FOOD

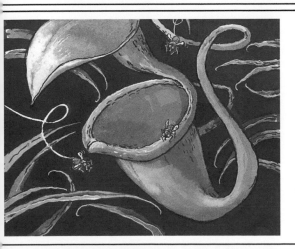

Nitrogen is one of the most important plant nutrients. Plants use nitrogen in photosynthesis, respiration, growth, and reproduction. Most plants get their nitrogen from rotting plants and animal poop in the soil.

Some plants live where there is a shortage of this stinky matter. Carnivorous plants "eat" insects to boost their nitrogen intake. They trap their prey using sticky gunk, pools of digestive juices, and trap doors.

17

CHAPTER 3

FLOWERS AND FRUITS

A dormant seed sleeps in the soil. The hard, outer seed coat hides an embryo waiting to grow. The seed also holds food for the embryo called endosperm.

The seed needs a wake-up call to grow. First, water seeps through the seed coat. When the temperature, light, and oxygen levels are just right, the seed germinates, meaning it starts to grow.

The plant matures and flowers. Through reproduction, the flowers make seeds.

The germinating seed begins the plant's life cycle. Soon a sprout pokes through the ground. The seedling grows above and below the soil.

The seeds scatter and wait to grow.

For some plants, a life cycle lasts a single year. This annual plant has run its full cycle. Since spring, it matured, bloomed, scattered seeds, and died.

Other plants have longer life cycles. Perennial plants sleep in the winter. Underground, their roots still take in water and nutrients.

In the spring, they wake up. New leaves bud on branches. New shoots burst up from the roots.

FACT A spruce tree in Sweden claims the title as oldest living tree. Scientists believe it is 9,550 years old.

When a plant grows up, it's ready to make baby plants. Most plants reproduce by spreading seeds. Some plants send out shoots that create new plants.

For most plants, the secret to reproduction is found in their flowers. Brightly colored petals draw attention to the plant's male and female parts.

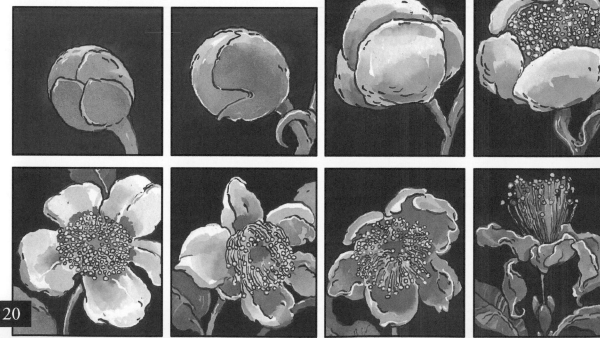

PISTIL **STAMEN**

OVULES

OVARY

The female part of the plant is called the pistil. Deep inside the pistil, the plant hides future seeds called ovules within its ovary.

The male part of the plant looks like an insect's antenna. The stamen has a pollen-filled sac.

Making a seed is tricky. Pollen must get from the stamen of one flower to the pistil of another. This process is called pollination. Then, an ovule becomes a seed with an embryo inside.

OVULES

SEEDS

FACT
Not all plants produce flowers and seeds. Ferns release dustlike spores. A fern may release millions of spores before one new fern grows.

Flowering plants need help for pollination. They lure insects and other animals with showy, scented flowers. Some flowers also offer sweet nectar. As visitors brush past the stamens, sticky pollen hitches a ride from flower to flower.

Some plants attract surprising pollinators. Banana plants lure bats to pollinate their flowers. At night, their large, pale flowers open with strong, fruity scents that attract the bats.

Other plants have no need for showy, scented flowers. They throw their pollen to the wind.

Some of the dry pollen finds its way to the plant's pistil. But most of it coats the area like dust.

SKUNK CABBAGE

Not all flowers smell sweet. Skunk cabbage flowers smell like rotting meat, which attracts carrion flies. Skunk cabbages have an internal heating system that can melt the snow around its spring flower. A skunk cabbage flower can be as much as 36° F (20° C) warmer than the air around it.

Once mature, plant seeds are ready for a home in the soil. The seeds need to find a way to get there.

Some seeds fly. Wispy dandelion seeds soar on the wind. Winged maple seeds flutter down from the tree.

Some plants bribe animals for help. They wrap their seeds in pretty, tasty fruits or berries. Many seeds are eaten whole. Once they're pooped out, the seeds have a new home and nutrients to help them grow.

This chipmunk collects seeds for a winter meal. But he's also helping spread the walnut tree's seeds. In spring, the uneaten seeds sprout into new trees.

Some plants get really sneaky. They pack their seeds in dry, barbed fruit. The barbs latch on to unsuspecting passers-by. These visitors carry the seeds to new homes.

FACT Some plants are explosive. They shoot their seeds out of their pods. Witch hazel shoots its seeds 30 to 40 feet (9 to 12 meters).

CHAPTER 4

THE VALUE OF PLANTS

Plants hold a special place in the world. Their ability to turn sunlight into food places them at the base of most food chains.

A food chain shows how energy moves from one living thing to another through food. A blade of grass starts a food chain. A grasshopper breakfasts on the grass. A mouse lunches on the grasshopper. The mouse then becomes dinner for a hawk.

No one wants to eat the same thing all the time. Animals are no different. Often, they compete with each other for food. A food web shows the connections between many different food chains.

In food chains and food webs, plants are the producers. They capture sunlight and turn it into food. Animals are consumers. They either eat plants or other animals that eat plants.

One way or another, every animal on the planet depends on plants for survival.

Plants aren't just food. People use plants for many things. Lumber from trees frame buildings and form furniture.

Plants hide fibers inside their stems and roots. People use these fibers to make paper and thread. Woven threads become comfy clothes and sheets.

Plants help keep people healthy and clean. Plant extracts make healing medicines. Plant oils and juices make soaps, lotions, and household cleaners.

You might not always realize it, but plants have many secrets. They make the world livable. They replace carbon dioxide in the air with oxygen. They produce food. They provide materials for clothing and shelter.

This tree is lucky. It found a home with plenty of space and sunlight. And it found some good friends who help it survive and grow.

GLOSSARY

cell (SEL)—the smallest unit of a living thing

chlorophyll (KLOR-uh-fil)—the green substance in plants that uses light to make food from carbon dioxide and water

dormant (DOR-muhnt)—not active

embryo (EM-bree-oh)—a plant in its first stage of development

germinate (jur-muh-NAYT)—when a seed sends out a root and a stem

glucose (GLOO-kose)—a natural sugar found in plants that gives energy to living things

nutrient (NOO-tree-uhnt)—a substance needed by a living thing to stay healthy

organelle (or-guh-NELL)—a small structure in a cell that performs a specific function and is surrounded by its own membrane

photosynthesis (foh-toh-SIN-thuh-siss)—a process plants use to make food and oxygen

pollination (pol-uh-NAY-shuhn)—the process of pollen moving from the male part of a flower to the female part

reproduction (ree-pruh-DUCT-shuhn)—the process by which a plant creates new plants

respiration (ress-puh-RAY-shuhn)—the process by which sugar stored in a plant is changed into energy; during respiration plants take in oxygen and send out carbon dioxide

tissue (TISH-yoo)—a mass of cells that form a certain part or organ of a person, animal, or plant

transpiration (transs-puh-RAY-shuhn)—the process by which plants pass water from the soil into the atmosphere

READ MORE

Hirsch, Rebecca E. *Science Lab: The Life Cycles of Plants*. Science Lab. Ann Arbor, Mich.: Cherry Lake Pub., 2011.

Levine, Shar. *Plants: Flowering Plants, Ferns, Mosses, and Other Plants*. A Class of Their Own. New York: Crabtree Pub., 2010.

Morgan, Sally. *The Plant Cycle*. Nature's Cycles. New York: Rosen Pub. Group's PowerKids Press, 2009.

Taylor, Barbara. *Inside Plants*. Invisible Worlds. New York: Marshall Cavendish Benchmark, 2010.

INTERNET SITES

FactHound offers a safe, fun way to find Internet sites related to this book. All of the sites on FactHound have been researched by our staff.

Here's all you do:

Visit www.facthound.com

Type in this code: 9781429676861

Check out projects, games and lots more at
www.capstonekids.com

INDEX